Deserts

Written by Tess Schembri
Series Consultant: Linda Hoyt

WorldWise™
Content-based Learning

Contents

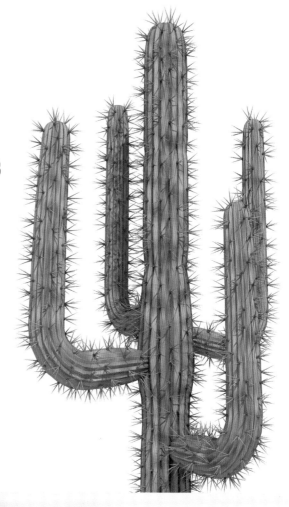

Introduction

Shut your eyes. Now imagine what a desert looks like. What are you seeing? A hot, dry sandy place where no trees or plants grow? That is what most of us think.

We often think of deserts as extremely hot, dry places covered in sand dunes. But although all deserts are dry, only a small number of the world's deserts are hot and sandy.

Some deserts are covered with mountains, some are very rocky, and some are freezing cold and covered in ice and snow. What all these places have in common is that they have very little rain.

 Did you know?

The Antarctic desert is one of the driest places on Earth. It has less than 20 centimetres of rain per year. But the Antarctic desert contains about 90 per cent of the earth's freshwater. This water is found in the permanently frozen ice sheet.

The Gobi Desert, Mongolia

The Perito Moreno Glacier in Patagonia, Argentina

Zabriskie Point, Death Valley National Park, California, USA

Different kinds of deserts

Deserts are found on every continent. They cover around 20 per cent of Earth. The largest deserts are not hot; they are freezing cold and are located at the North and South Poles.

Ten largest deserts

	Desert	Area in square kilometres	Type
1	Antarctic	8,800,000	Polar desert
2	Arctic	8,700,000	Polar desert
3	Sahara	5,600,000	Subtropical desert
4	Arabian	1,800,000	Subtropical desert
5	Gobi	800,000	Inland cold desert
6	Patagonian	420,000	Cold rain shadow desert
7	Great Victoria	400,000	Subtropical desert
8	Kalahari	350,000	Subtropical desert
9	Great Basin	300,000	Cold rain shadow desert
10	Syrian	300,000	Subtropical desert

North America

9

South Am

6

Deserts are formed in different ways. Very little rain falls in deserts – less than 25 centimetres of rain each year.

They are hard places for plants and animals to survive, but some plants and animals have made each type of desert their home.

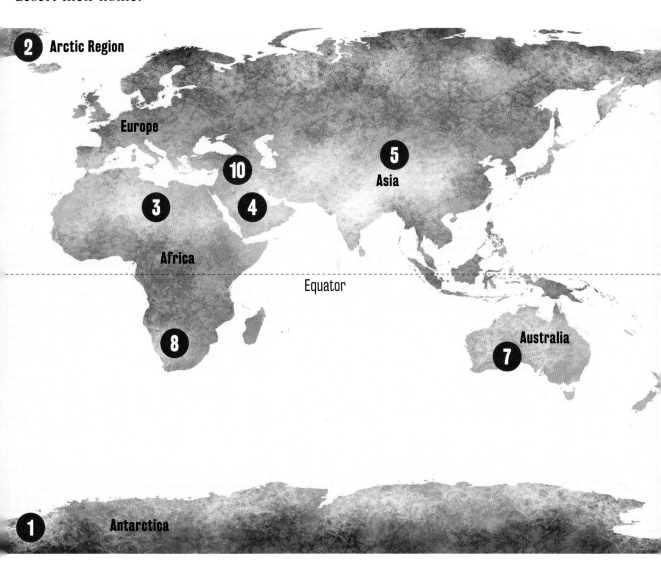

2 Arctic Region

Europe

10

3

5
Asia

4

Africa

Equator

8

Australia

7

1 Antarctica

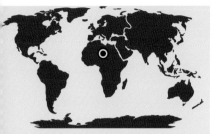

- Location:
  northern Africa
- Hottest daytime
  temperature:
  over 50 degrees
  Celsius
- Nighttime
  temperature:
  down to 0 degrees
  Celsius

The Sahara
– a subtropical desert

The Sahara is a hot, dry desert. The Nile and the Niger are the two permanent rivers in this vast landscape. Some water is available from smaller underground storage places, and some drains from the mountains.

About four million people live in the Sahara. Many of these people are **nomads** who move from place to place, but others live in villages and cities, such as Cairo in Egypt.

The Hoggar Mountains in central Sahara, Algeria.
The Sahara is dotted with sand dunes, but most of it is made up of barren, hard, rocky plateaus and mountains.

Animals of the Sahara

Mammals	Jerboa, fennec fox, jackal, hyena, camel, goat, screw-horn antelope
Birds	Finch, silverbill, ostrich, bee-eater, owl, raven
Reptiles	Sand viper, monitor lizard, chameleon, skink, cobra
Invertebrates	Deathstalker scorpion, ants

Deathstalker scorpion

The deathstalker is considered the most dangerous scorpion in the world. It feeds on spiders and insects, which it hunts at night, when it is cooler. This helps the scorpion survive.

How do subtropical deserts form?

The Sahara is a subtropical desert. These deserts are found near the Equator and are formed by hot, dry winds.

1. Warm moist air rises at the Equator. As the air rises, it cools and forms clouds. Lots of rain falls from the clouds at the Equator, leaving the air dry.

2. Dry warm air moves away from the Equator to the areas north and south of the Equator – the tropics. This is where many deserts can be found.

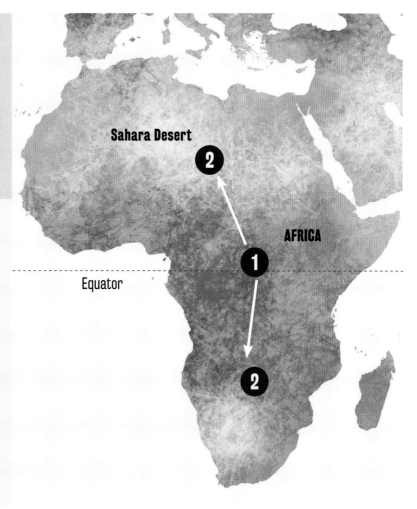

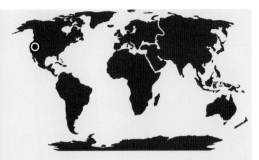

- Location: eastern California near the border of Nevada
- Temperature: up to 56 degrees Celsius in summer
- Average rainfall: 6 centimetres per year

Death Valley
– a rain shadow desert

Death Valley is one of the hottest places in the world. It is made up of sand dunes, mountains, springs, ponds and **salt pans** from dried-up lakes. Parts of Death Valley are at the lowest level in North America at 85 metres below sea level. Native Americans called the Timbisha made their home in the valley.

Zabriskie Point is a part of Amargosa Range located east of Death Valley in the Death Valley National Park, in California, USA.

Animals of Death Valley

Mammals	Bighorn sheep, pronghorn antelope, coyote, bobcat, bat, gopher, kangaroo rat, fox, badger
Birds	Red-tailed hawk, roadrunner, shrike
Reptiles	Desert tortoise, sidewinder rattlesnake, zebra-tailed lizard
Invertebrates	Snails, leeches, worms, spiders

Greater roadrunner

Roadrunners belong to the cuckoo family. These birds can survive in the desert because they eat animals and plants that have a high water content. These birds hunt during the day. They are fast runners – they can run at speeds up to 27 kilometres per hour – and can fly to escape **predators**.

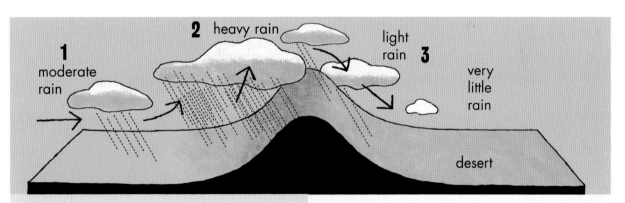

1 moderate rain

2 heavy rain

light rain **3**

very little rain

desert

How do rain shadow deserts form?

Death Valley is on the dry side of the Sierra Nevada mountain range. The dry side of a mountain range is called the rain shadow. Deserts are often found near large mountains and are formed by rain shadows.

1. The wind blows warm, moist air towards a mountain range.

2. The air is pushed up the mountain slopes and cools, forming clouds. As the clouds are pushed higher up the mountains, they lose their moisture as rain.

3. When the air reaches the other side of the mountain, it is dry.

11

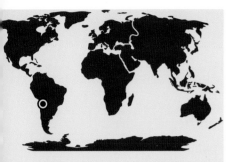

The Atacama Desert

– a coastal desert

- Location:
  Chile, South America
- Temperature:
  40 degrees Celsius
  during the day;
  4 degrees Celsius
  at night
- Average rainfall:
  3–15 millimetres
  per year

The Atacama Desert is one of the driest deserts in the world. It is the oldest desert on Earth, and at 2,200 metres above sea level, it is one of the highest deserts.

This desert has a varied landscape that includes mountains, volcanoes, canyons, geysers, lakes, salt flats, sand dunes and stony, rocky hills. Thousands of years ago, South American native people called the Chinchorro lived in the Atacama. In more recent times, the Inca people moved into the area.

The Valley of the Moon,
Atacama Desert, Chile

Animals of the Atacama

Mammals	Darwin's leaf-eared mouse, grey fox, culpeo fox	
Birds	Giant hummingbird, flamingo, sparrow	
Reptiles	Atacama toad, iguana, lava lizard	
Invertebrates	Beetle, desert wasp, red scorpion, sand-coloured grasshopper	

Andean flamingo

Three species of flamingo live in the Atacama. Flamingos get their food and water from the shallow lakes that are fed by rivers. They feed on the bottom layer of shallow water, and mainly eat tiny plants that grow in the water.

How do coastal deserts form?

Chile's huge Atacama Desert is a coastal desert that is in a rain shadow from the Andes Mountains. **Cold currents** that run along the western edges of many continents cool the air along their coastlines. This cooler air is unable to hold much moisture.

Any moisture that it does hold usually falls on the ocean before the rain hits the land. Fog is often a feature of the climate in coastal deserts.

Equator

SOUTH AMERICA

Atacama

Cold currents

ANDES

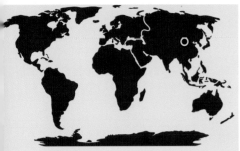

- Location:
  southern Mongolia/
  northwestern China
- Temperature:
  45 degrees Celsius in
  summer; –4 degrees
  Celsius in winter
- Average rainfall:
  19 centimetres per year

The Gobi Desert
– an inland desert

The fifth largest desert in the world is the Gobi. It is a cold desert. In some parts of the Gobi, it is so cold that the sand dunes are covered with frost and snow in winter.

In summer, it can be extremely hot. Strong dry winds blow across this desert, exposing a rocky landscape. It has mountains, salt ponds and sand dunes.

Today, traditional Mongol nomads live in the Gobi, where they farm sheep, goats, camels and horses.

Sand dunes in the Gobi Desert

Camels are led through sand dunes in the Gobi Desert.

Animals of the Gobi

Mammals	Przewalski's horse, jerboa, snow leopard, grey wolf, black-tailed gazelle
Birds	Golden eagle, demoiselle crane, kite, magpie, vulture
Reptiles	Central Asian pit viper, plate-tailed gecko, Mongolian toad, steppe rat snake
Invertebrates	Desert tarantula, scorpion, ant, centipede, beetle

Plate-tailed gecko

This small reptile lives in deep holes to protect itself from the heat and cold. It hunts at night for flying insects and other desert insects and smaller animals.

How do inland deserts form?

The Gobi Desert in Mongolia is far from any ocean and is called an inland desert.

Inland deserts form in areas that are a long way from the oceans. Air close to oceans collects moisture. As the moist air moves over land, it cools and forms clouds. By the time the air has travelled a long way inland, it has often lost all its moisture and is dry.

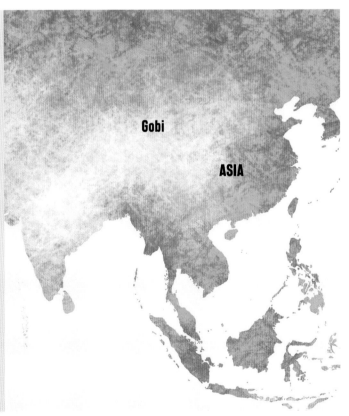

Gobi

ASIA

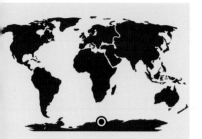

- Location:
  Antarctica
- Temperature:
  –53 degrees
  Celsius
- Average rainfall:
  20 centimetres
  per year

Antarctica
– a polar desert

The largest desert in the world is Antarctica. You might not think of Antarctica as a desert, but it has an average rainfall of 20 centimetres per year. Although there are huge amounts of water in Antarctica, it is all frozen in glaciers, icebergs and sea ice. This makes it a desert as there is little water available for plants and animals.

Few living things can survive the freezing dry climate of Antarctica. No animals are able to spend the entire year on the Antarctic continent. Some birds spend part of the year on the land to breed and raise their young. Marine animals thrive in the seas around the continent, but only a few tiny invertebrates – animals without backbones – are able to survive on the land.

Snowfields in Antarctica

Animals of Antarctica

Mammals	Leopard seal, elephant seal, whale, dolphin
Birds	Emperor penguin, wandering albatross, skua, tern, gull
Reptiles	None
Invertebrates	Krill in the waters, mites and worms on the land

Krill
The water surrounding Antarctica is home to millions of small shrimp-like animals called krill. Many animals feed on krill.

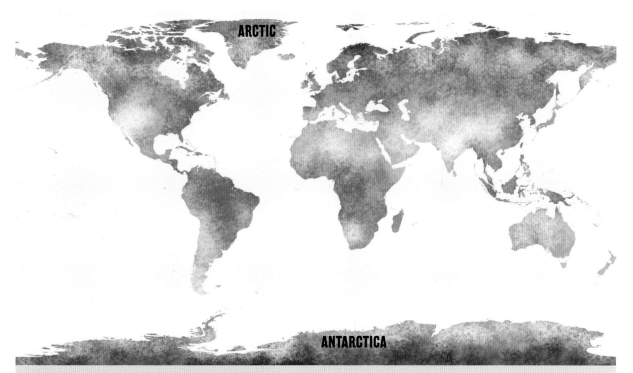

ARCTIC

ANTARCTICA

How do polar deserts form?

Polar deserts are found in the Arctic and Antarctica. These places are the coldest places on Earth and are freezing cold all year. The air is so cold, it is dry and holds no moisture. For this reason, there is less than 25 centimetres of rain per year in polar deserts.

Plant survivors

Hewitt Canyon, Arizona, USA

Plants have also developed in many different ways that allow them to survive in deserts. We call this **adaptation**.

Evading the drought

Some desert plants survive by appearing only after rain. They are called annuals because they live for one season. A desert can change into a wonderland of flowers almost overnight when soaking rain comes.

Before the rain

After the rain

Did you know?

The saguaro cactus is the largest cactus in the USA. It can grow to over 20 metres tall and weigh more than five tonnes.

Adapting to drought

Desert soil is often rocky and unable to hold much water. Strong, dry winds can cause plants to lose moisture and dry out. Plants that live in deserts have developed many ways to prevent drying out.

One group of plants that has adapted to life in a desert is called **succulents**. These plants store water in their stems and leaves. A waxy coating on the stem helps reduce water loss.

The cactus plant is a succulent. Large cactus plants have long root systems that spread out to collect water when it is available. This water is stored in the stem. Sharp spines on the stems discourage animals from eating the plant to get water.

Cactus flowers open at night to attract insects and other animals that are active when it is cooler. These animals move pollen from plant to plant so that the cactuses can make fruits and seeds.

Sharp spikes on a cactus stop animals from eating it.

Desert plants flower after it rains.

A solitary cactus bee collects pollen from a cactus flower even though the sun has gone down.

Some desert plants have hairs on their leaves that help shade the plant and reduce water loss. Other desert plants have leaves that turn throughout the day to expose a smaller surface area to the heat.

Plants use water when they make food using the sun's energy. Desert plants often grow very slowly, so they need less food. This means that they use less energy and less water.

Sturt's desert pea grows in the Great Victoria Desert in Australia. The leaves and stems are covered with a thick mat of short hairs that form a blanket over the plant to protect it from heat and cold.

Often in a desert, plants grow far apart. Their roots are close to the surface, but spread out over a large area so they can take in water when rain falls. This allows each plant to collect more water. This spacing makes some desert regions look like there is little life, but it also allows desert plants to trap enough water.

Great Victoria Desert, Australia. Plants grow far apart so they have a better chance of collecting water when it rains.

Animal survivors

Desert animals have developed a huge range of ways of adapting to the **arid**, hot and cold conditions of the desert. Some even seek out extreme places to raise their young. Deserts limit the size of both individual animals and animal populations.

Avoiding the heat

Many animals that live in hot deserts are **nocturnal**, sleeping during the day and coming out at night when the temperatures are cooler. These nocturnal animals have bodily features that help them live in dark places.

Animals that are not so well adapted to life in the dark hunt at daybreak and just before dusk when conditions are cooler.

The colouring and shape of the Australian barking gecko makes it very hard to see at night. They have large eyes that allow them to see in dim light so they can find food.

Bobcats are most active at dusk and dawn. When they are not active, they rest in cool places such as hollow logs, caves, rocky dens or some other covered shelter.

How animals adapt to desert conditions

Adaptation	Animals	What they do
Avoiding the heat	Barking gecko, elf owl	Hunt at night
	Bobcat, Kenyan sand boa	Hunt at daybreak or dusk
Burrows and hollows	Spinifex hopping mouse, tortoises, foxes, snakes, lizards, rodents	Rest in cool places or under the ground
Losing heat	Bilby, fennec fox	Have very large ears
Getting water	Thorny devil, Namib desert beetle	Have body features that help them collect water
Storing water	Mojave desert tortoise	Has special body parts for storing water
Avoiding drought	Couch's spadefoot toad, African bullfrog, Australian burrowing frogs	Burrow underground and stay there for long periods until conditions are right for breeding and feeding
Retaining heat	Emperor penguin, seals, whales	Have body coverings to keep the cold out and layers of fat to keep the heat in

The Kenyan sand boa is a small snake that stays buried under the surface of desert sands or under a rock. In the cool of the morning and evening, this snake emerges from its **lair** and seizes **prey** as they move past. It kills small prey by dragging them under the sand where they cannot breathe. It then crushes them with its body.

Burrows and hollows

Small animals such as insects, spiders and scorpions live in many desert environments. Most of these small animals escape the heat during the day by hiding in rocky **crevices** or underground holes.

Desert tortoises, rodents, foxes and scorpions are some of the many animals that spend their days sleeping in underground burrows.

The elf owl is a tiny bird that you might not expect to see in a desert. These tiny owls are about 12 centimetres tall. They escape the heat of the day by resting in **cavities** in saguaro cactus plants that have been made and abandoned by woodpeckers. Elf owls also use these cavities to nest and raise their young.

At night, elf owls hunt, using their excellent night vision and sharp hearing. They capture and eat moths, crickets, scorpions, centipedes and beetles. Like many desert animals, they get enough water from the food they eat to survive in places without surface water.

The elf owl is found in parts of the Sonoran Desert, southwestern USA. These tiny owls are about 12 centimetres tall.

Bilbys are found in sand country across Australian deserts. They are marsupials that feed on plants and small animals.

The fennec fox has large ears and furry paws.

Losing heat

A few desert animals have body parts that enable them to live in hot deserts.

Bilbys have large paper-thin ears with lots of tiny blood vessels near the surface of the skin. This allows heat to escape into the air and helps cool their bodies. The nocturnal feeders get most of the water they need from the plants they eat.

Fennec foxes live in the Sahara desert in North Africa. These small foxes have huge batlike ears. Not only do their large ears help them hear prey, they also help them stay cool in the scorching daytime heat. They also have fur on their paws, which protects their feet from the hot desert sand.

 Find out more

What other mammals can live in deserts? What body features do they have that enable them to survive?

A fog rolls in from the ocean over the Namib desert. This desert is next to the ocean on the west coast of Africa.

A Namib desert beetle

A Namib desert beetle lifting its body to capture moisture

Did you know?
Less than 3 centimetres of rain falls in the Namib desert in Africa each year. But each morning, a fog blows in from the Atlantic Ocean. The droplets of water in this fog provide moisture to the Namib desert.

Getting water

Most animals that live in deserts either store water in their bodies or get their water needs met by the foods they eat.

A beetle that lives in the Namib desert in southern Africa has a unique way of getting water. This beetle lives on the sand dunes and can survive on very little water. It has a specially adapted shell with bumps and ridges that can capture water vapour from the air.

When a fog blows in from the ocean, this beetle stands on the top of a dune facing the wind. It lowers its head and raises its back. The bumps on its shell capture moisture from the fog, which runs down the ridges and into its mouth.

Storing water

Some animals, such as Gila monsters, store water in fatty deposits in their tails or other tissue.

Mojave desert tortoises have a secret to survival hidden inside their hard, dry shells. This **adaptation** is an oversized bladder that can carry extra water. It can carry over one litre of water, plus waste items from its body. In wet conditions, these reptiles drink a great deal of extra water to store in their bladders.

Mojave desert tortoises avoid the heat and limit the amount of water they need by living in burrows and **hibernating** for part of the year.

Gila monster

Mojave desert tortoise

The Mojave desert tortoise drinking water from a shallow pond

27

Couch's
spadefoot toad

Avoiding the drought

Some amphibians have found ways of avoiding the dry, hot desert climate. Australia has several species and some of these live in deserts. They spend most of their lives buried under the ground and are only active during floods or heavy rains.

As soon as it rains, they are quick to breed and to eat. Their eggs are laid in shallow ponds and hatch very quickly. They need to grow from tadpoles into frogs within two weeks before the sun dries up their pond.

The new adults eat as many insects as they can before digging a burrow where it will hibernate until heavy rains or floods return.

The African bullfrog and the Couch's spade foot toad from southern USA and Mexico have a similar life cycle to the Australian burrowing frogs.

Spencers Burrowing frog

African bullfrog

Australian burrowing frog

The huddle is an essential behaviour for male Emperor penguins to reduce heat loss. Changing positions is important to share the heat.

After the female lays her egg, the male scoops it up onto his feet and covers it with his stomach skin and feathers.

Retaining heat

The biggest challenge for animals in polar deserts is to stay warm and not lose body heat. Only one large animal spends the winter in Antarctica – the Emperor penguin.

Emperor penguins have many body features that help them survive the freezing cold conditions. Two layers of feathers keep them warm and stop them from losing body heat. They also have a large amount of body fat that not only keeps them warm but also gives them energy. Small beaks and flippers reduce heat loss. Feathers on their legs stop their ankles from getting too chilly. And their feet contain special fats that prevent them from freezing while standing on ice.

Male Emperor penguins spend the dark winter many kilometres inland from the sea, looking after the eggs and raising their young. The males huddle together in a large group, taking turns to be in the middle of the huddle because it is much colder on the outside. Penguins would not survive on their own in the dark, cold Antarctic winter.

Find out more

Male Emperor penguins do not eat anything while caring for their eggs during the cold winter. For how long do they not eat during this time?

Conclusion

Around the world, many deserts are growing larger.

As the population of the world grows, people are moving into the areas around deserts and using them to grow crops or raise farm animals. These areas often have low rainfall of less than 50 millimetres per year. When animals graze on the native grasses, the soil is exposed. Strong winds blow the topsoil away. And when it does rain, even more soil is washed away. These areas may easily turn into deserts.

In the Gobi Desert, reed fencing is used to stop the sand from being blown away.

Feral animals are causing problems across Australian deserts. They compete with native animals for food and water.

In some countries, trees in **arid** areas are being cut down to provide wood for buildings, heating and firewood. In many places, wood is the only source of energy for cooking and heating. Cutting down trees and not replanting causes deforestation. The loss of plants that held the soil together causes soil erosion, and in these low rainfall, semi-arid areas, deserts are formed.

Glossary

adaptation the process of change over generations that enables animals to survive in particular conditions

arid having little or no rain

cavities empty spaces within a solid object such as a plant or rock

cold currents currents that move cold water from the polar regions towards the equator

crevices narrow openings in rocks

hibernating becoming inactive throughout winter, by slowing down body systems

lair a place where a wild animal lives

nocturnal active at nighttime

nomads people who travel from place to place to find fresh pasture for their animals; they set up homes in the places where their animals graze

predators animals that get food by killing and eating other animals

prey an animal that is caught and eaten by another animal

salt pans a shallow area on the ground where there was once seawater; when the seawater evaporates, salt is left behind

succulents plants that have thick, fleshy stems that help them retain water

Index